A Thistle Stuck in the Throat of the Sun

A Thistle Stuck in the Throat of the Sun

Poems by

Dane Hamann

Cover artwork by Andrew Slivka
Cover design by Shay Culligan
Photograph of the author by Jeana Platz

ISBN: 978-1-63980-006-3

Kelsay Books
502 South 1040 East, A-119
American Fork, Utah 84003
Kelsaybooks.com

For my family

Acknowledgments

The Sillitoe epigraph is from *The Loneliness of the Long-Distance Runner*.

The Shaw epigraph is from "Run Like Fire Once More" in Harper's Magazine (August 2007).

The Langemak epigraph is from "The History of Running" in Copper-Nickel (Fall 2016, Issue 23).

×

"Sailing Stones" is a found poem composed of text from Joseph Stromberg's article "How Do Death Valley's 'Sailing Stones' Move Themselves Across the Desert?" on Smithsonianmag.com.

The art deco mountains mentioned in "Light Splashing So Deliberately" refer to the architecture of Wicker Park, Chicago, specifically the "Coyote Building."

"Personal Best: New Mile" references a route that was run many Mondays with many close friends around Northfield and Dundas, Minnesota.

"Half Ghost" is a found poem composed of text from Alan Sillitoe's story *The Loneliness of the Long-Distance Runner*.

×

Earlier versions of several poems in this collection, sometimes with different titles, first appeared in the following journals:

Barren Magazine: "Hammer"
Black Fox Literary Magazine: "Half Ghost"
Calamus Journal: "Do You Blame the Morning for the Tendrils"

Cobalt Magazine: "Light Splashing So Deliberately"
COUNTERCLOCK Journal: "Pinhole Sunrise"
DASH Literary Journal: "High Water"
Door is a Jar: "Sailing Stones"
Figure 1: "A Saw into Cedar"
Ghost City Review: "Thoughts"
Half Mystic: "What Makes an Ordinary Thing Improbable?"
Harpur Palate: "Scrap"
Kissing Dynamite: "Ennui"
L'éphémère Review: "August"
Lily Poetry Review: "Distance"
Line + Stars: "Fifty-Two Card Pickup"
Nice Cage: "Tipping Point"
November Bees: "Do You Remember the Storm"
Parentheses Journal: "The Softest Things"
Porridge Magazine: "Rust," "Distance"
Recenter Press Journal: "Fields"
Riggwelter: "Ice Bright in the Harbor"
riverbabble: "Where Have Your Wanderings Finally Brought You?"
Switchback Journal: "Strange Factories," "Why Do We Bathe in Miles of Dust?"
The Night Heron Barks: "Thresholds"
Thin Air Magazine: "The Late Hours"
Two Peach: "Who Will Play the Song of Catastrophe"
Two Thirds North: "Lights"
Water~Stone Review: "Mill"
Wildness: "Will the Nearly Broken World Understand"
Willows Wept Review: "Snapped Collarbone," "On the Shore of the Lake, I Stare into the Midnight Sky"

The long poem "Tributaries" first appeared in *What the River Made,* a micro-chapbook in the 2018 Ghost City Press Micro-Chapbook Series.

Some poems in this collection also appeared in *Q & A,* a limited-edition chapbook published by Sutra Press.

Thank you to all of the editors who saw something in my poetry and wanted to share it with the world through their publications.

×

I am grateful to the following people who have helped me become a better writer and person.

My family, especially Jeana, who has always believed in my writing, and Maisie, who has inspired me from the moment she came into our lives.

My parents, who have always encouraged my artistic endeavors.

The faculty and staff of the Northwestern University MFA program for their dedication to poetry and learning. Reginald Gibbons for his attentiveness and insight into an early draft of this book. My fellow poets from the MFA program as well as my fellow editors and staff members of TriQuarterly, especially Dan Fliegel for our discussions about poetry and running.

All of the harriers, thinclads, and relay teammates who have raced or shared a run with me over the many years, especially Jason, Jesse, Marc, Sam, and Coach Thornton.

Thank you to Andrew Slivka (www.plumoriginals.com) for the use of his artwork for the cover.

Infinite gratitude to the Kelsay Books team.

Contents

III

I

Sometimes I think that I've never been so free as during that couple of hours when I'm trotting up the path out of the gates and turning by that bare-faced, big-bellied oak tree at the lane end.
—Alan Sillitoe

August

A wall of heat dances on the horizon.
It is late August in the prairieland
and everything is coming undone.
Along the shoulders of the road, rockets
of milkweed flare into cottony plumes.
Pollen as massive as north woods mosquitos
drifts from the fields across the two lanes.
The wind chops the long wavering note
of the cattail orchestra. More static plays
steadily in the gravel beneath my shoes.
The taste of asphalt melting in my throat,
I'm counting every light-peppered mile
that remains between us. But the stick-straight
road bestows only the notion of ending.

A Thistle

I'm a stitch pulled from the dust. A thistle
stuck in the throat of the sun. Smoke along the road.

How far must I go until my mouth spills
the alphabet of emptiness? I don't know

how many shadows I've sieved through skin.
My body forgives the light, but never these ghosts.

This I'll learn years from now
as I prepare once again to unspool hours

from myself. In that moment, I'll need you
to tell me that the salt of the body

comes from the cave of the heart. Then I'll go,
tongue at last finding the sound for a stone

carried in the shoe of a river of flesh.
Every word for further and further.

Mill

We drape ourselves over
a footbridge, arms vined

between truss beams,
as swift waters braid

our reflections. The river
tumbles past an empty mill

on the far bank. Generations
of fine flour long since washed

away. A new floor of black dirt
and a shoot-and-sapling scramble

curling against roofless
stonework. A few iron ends,

carbonized tokens from doused
cigarette fires, still linger

wedged in ruined walls.
The mill, a tree-bound house

of wind, no longer speaks of
labor, only of the harshness

of seasons. That the mill seems
more ancient than the river

is the river's nature. The current
always renewing the water,

and the water renewing us
simply by flowing as it's flowed

for ages through this valley. Here
we stretch and are stretched,

watch each other pour again
and again across river stones,

leaving only when our skin
is wild with high-noon sweat.

A Saw into Cedar

The roar of the highway is not unlike
a nest of bees fed to me. Electric

in the way my hands numb into humming
shards. Filling in the way that loneliness

sometimes runs like a ribbon of asphalt,
a thousand miles of an unwrapped shadow.

Inside us there are deep, unclaimed spaces
only accessible along the wild

shoulders of roads. I'll unwrap like a field
of wheat from a rock. That's stopwatch logic.

Or maybe that's equilibrium. No
one thing greater than another out here:

the wind puts its fists to my lungs and I
cut through it like a saw into cedar.

Scrap

Squint-dizzy in the hallways of summer,
I lean into the unquenchable hands

of the sun as it heaps the rollicking
industry of daytime over me: heat

and the nova-flash of glass and metal,
motorcycle Doppler songs, the far-off

shirt-rip of mower engines, radios
generously pushing their waves toward

the shore of me. This unroofed factory
floor, this place of sweat, where all things are made

by the unmaking of something else. See
me there among the workpieces? I'm simply

scrap cast from the spinning lathe of warm light,
waiting to find form in these dusty hours.

Distance

The edge of sky is a door closed to us.
We eat the dry grief of distance like beasts,
wind-worn gazelles, teeth gleaming below thin
November clouds, untouched by fear or need
for escape from that which long chases us—
a lifetime of never crossing the bridge
connecting what we've already done to what
we could do. Truth hidden if not in our marrow,
then somewhere along the ridgelines of salt
building on our bodies. We are trying
to remember human gestures. Trying
to sing our names to the road, our mouths caked
with hunger and ash. We allow ourselves
a feast of air—cannot speak the word full.

Given a Garden, Would You Stitch

the earth back together with roots and bulbs,
and leave the clay in the teeth of mountains?
I've always thought it is better to share
the language of sun-split vegetables
than of brick. I'd rather let a brushfire
burn the figure eight of a drained hourglass
into our tongues than imprison our sense
of astonishment when the soft light flows
from an unbarricaded horizon.
Yes, our throats will fill with smoke and cinders.
Our skin will sugar in the heat. Still,
we'll feed seeds into the dirt. Shake lake
water from our pores. Given a garden,
we could speak again in our wildest tones.

Sailing Stones

There is no evidence this is magic—
this landscape, this collar of gravel roads.
It's quiet. The field seems like a tabletop,
the pavement like a lakebed. Trees the size
of canyons. The hours glide like sheets of ice.
Miles are scattered like torn paper, mountains
of wind blowing in zigzagging devils.

There is a mystery though—we are stones,
but escaped from that existence. We move
across this place, this bone-rattling racetrack,
propelled by some absurd magnetism. Soaked
in dust, sun, and time. It's an unanswered
question—one lost to the harsh furnace of
movement. We are endlessly locked to it.

Hammer

I worry the hammer writing its bite
in a script of bruises doesn't distinguish

between fiction and prayer. I don't ask
for much. Sunlight more like bed than whip

of gold. Or, in the afternoon, whisky
drizzle instead of a sky-shredded soak.

I ask that the hinges of my body
swing as smooth as a wet tongue over teeth.

These things don't always come to pass. Instead
I learn that most times all the hammer tells

is distance. A long, long story of me
shredding myself and finally learning

to ask you to gather me as if I
were petals in the rush of a cold stream.

Spring

Very little lasts in the sweet-smelling
spring. Acid-etched metals show a cosmos
of rain's needlework. It seems this bleeding
sticks to me too, and I no longer feel
like my body is a bold stroke across
the ochre and steel landscape. The toothed sound
of my movement saws into the quiet
puddle of air. My bones willow and bite.
My lungs are a workshop. The thing is, I
want to be both engine and earth. The cage
of technology and the bower of
infinite color. So as my legs turn
like seasons, every bruise greens. I carry
these marks into the gray world, plant them there.

Thresholds

Our shadows stretch as tall as pines.

The energy of the day slowly dissipates.
We're searching the rooms of ourselves

for one more mirror to mistake for a window.

Every threshold is a fulcrum.
We tip to one side and night descends

like the thirsty into a dry riverbed.

We lean to the other side and the sun
continues to burn so bright it siphons

all of the air from us. We're unbalanced,

fitful moths, one wing dipped in cast iron,
the other fragile velvet, wavering

like grass before the edge of a wildfire.

When Our Words Come in Rushes of Wind

and snap branches from our tongues, do we
let them lie like pieces of ossified lightning

in the grass? Or do we haul them homeward?
We could plant them under floorboards.

Pull them into our beds. Weave them
between tables and chairs. The sapwood

is not yet too dry. Every meal, branches
would beg at our feet. We'd unlatch

the shutters to let rain dance along the walls,
let our home grow like a slick valley

floor. We'd tear holes in the ceiling
to better hear thunder. Fists reddening

against sheetrock, feet re-mapping
every road run with gypsum powder.

Tufts of fiberglass would flower
in our hair. We might finally learn,

raw and roofless, the words for every
spoonful of sweat we've fed to the trees.

That the sound of stepping on dried bark
is simply our crackling thirst.

Thoughts

Thinking—not blood.
The machine of the heart

slips into sequence
with the percussion

of feet on road,
the sunset orangish-red.

Not thinking of friction
or fluid, the thrum

of living. But I'm
alive. I'm thinking—

I will be found
wind-eaten and, at least,

sun-perfumed
from collecting dusty miles

like pennies in a swear jar.
I'm thinking—

this may be beautiful,
this unending

echo in every chamber
of me. This

is me pulling knives out
of my flawed soul.

This is me lighter than
an eyelash, veins

pulsing with air.
I'm thinking—I'm bleeding.

My thoughts drain
into the red horizon.

Fifty-Two Card Pickup

The aluminum dock groans
as it returns to knife-blade

coolness in the August-seared
bowl of a prairie lake. My mind

plays fifty-two card pickup
with the scattered hours

as the low creak of conversation
weaves between tree branches

and screen doors. The night
is strewn about to fade and melt

in the embers of a bonfire snapping
defiantly at a soup of stars.

A hunger burns too, first
in the far-off hollowness

of thigh bones, then right above
the heart. A need to consume

shadows and drink up the obsidian
slab of lake water, to find and file

every hidden thing within the raked
coals of these passing moments.

Honeyed Gravel

In the narrow tunnel of my vision,
the sky and road meet at a whirlpool
of light swallowing honeyed gravel
by the tongueful. Along the hilltop
crawls a silhouette of barbed wire.

The doors within me have been flung
so far open they've come off their hinges.
It's good then that I can at least
recognize a route has been designed,
that there are places not meant for me.

The sailing stones that skim across
the flat mirror of an otherwise empty
valley go only where the wind pushes them.
I believe there must be something left
within me that can catch this breeze.

Tracks

A beating ocean short minutes ago,
my heart drums muddy fire along the paved
rail line. The old tracks ran dead into sun
or away from it. Today, frost glints deep
in my eyes as I head toward sunset,
testing my heavy legs. Shadows grow blue.
I feel like tortured clay. I'm not sure when
I'll turn, doubling back to the trailhead lot.
The plank and iron suture no longer
under my feet used to be a simple
distance over which things were carried. Now
it carries only my desire to rest
or be made of a younger self. The smooth
set asphalt as unforgiving as me.

Rust

Rust flowers behind my eyes. Little stars
blooming, then melting like spittle into

soft earth. A wheelbarrow bearing water,
I must not lose too much of myself when

the cup of the past thirsts for me. I fill
it first with the lead pouring down my neck

in church-bell slugs, then with the whitewater
pinning me within myself. I fill it

with pools of light gathering in acres
of shoeprints. Sometimes the cup is shallow.

A pinhole filled by the feathery gasp
of soft exhaustion. Other times, the cup

voices a deep drought. I cannot give it
enough and there is so much left to give.

Light Splashing So Deliberately

I'm through the door and into a ravine
of storefronts. Lonely delivery vans

lumber out of sight, their fat tires
screeching around corners. Pans clatter

behind a screen door, bakery aroma
drifting into the early morning dust.

A taste of the lake on the breeze.
Lavender light softens spasms of neon

from the sidewalks. The brightest
remnants from last night are stained

leaflets fluttering against telephone poles.
A train clatters emptily down the line

away from the city. Masses of vine-like
wires crackle now and then overhead.

The very bricks of the buildings course
with invisible electrons. I'm magnetized.

Between slices of sky, old towers loom like art
deco mountains and pull me to their shadows.

There, where the sun hasn't yet reached
and the air is still cool, hollow newspaper

machines colonize star-shaped intersections.
Sunrise begins to pool along the windows

of a chalk-white high-rise. And yet,
this seems the extent of the world:

blocks of humming, bolt-locked buildings,
light splashing so deliberately below

my feet. My only choice being to alleyway
into the gentle, graffitied fuzz of the day.

Personal Best: New Mile

It's easy to forget
the build of these feet,

like the wings of migratory birds
I sometimes praise

as if they weren't mine,
when the hiss and sigh

of each stride
becomes the swallowing breeze.

First the bready air
around the Malt-O-Meal factory

turns sweet with leaf decay,
pools of old rainwater.

Then I forget somewhere
along County Road 78

how to count anything
besides my desires.

I want to rest.
I want to be told

to rest.
But instead, I break

across the loose quartzite
ballast of railroad track,

heaviness seeping
from muscle into bone,

my eyes focusing for the first time
on the faded afternoon

sky and the distant line
of trees

that marks my frontier.
A silvery shine

creeps at the edges of my vision,
and the notion of stopping

hurtles through me.
It is enough

to cast doubt over the entire journey.
But just as a ragged edge

begins to be torn in each breath,
I find that I've crossed that border of trees

and I'm gulping
unknown air and light.

Summer Sweetening

Hot night. Streetlamps spilling bugs
     like a bonfire spits out sparks. So many

songs that aren't music punctuating
     the dark. Unseen instruments rasping

away in the grass. The clock slowed
     by the soupy air. Sweat beautiful along

the spine. Shins egg-shelled by morning
     miles. Eyes adjusted to the way trees

touch the nocturnal sky. Doorways shining.
     Their brightness, islands. The whole

walk here, a tunnel to a different light.
     Steel and pink evening still pouring

from the body. An unempty cup. Desire is
     a summer sweetening water into liquor.

What Makes an Ordinary Thing Improbable?

No one ever said
we could untether

every anchor from ourselves

and become like the wind
across open water.

But just today,

I found myself moving
through the woods

as if I were coming home to you
after a night of passing over

a calm, green sea.

I followed smudges of neon
cast from some place within me,

as if I were a jukebox of nothing but waves.

I never believed
that I could contain both

the light that shapes mountains
and the tar that spoils
each new moon.

I never learned the difference

between the steady murmur of your breath
and the parade of water
trampling the land,

ceaseless songs played by the wind.

No one ever really listens

to the music that fills
the smallest spaces between us.

It's mad to think
that either the earth or the sea

care how far we travel
to unlock ourselves.

There, in the woods,
it was not a key or a quarter

but a simple blade of want
that I pressed into myself.

It was raining,

and you seemed so sharp
compared to the trees rolling like the sea.

Morning

The night fractures into day,
brittle and vast. Again, the frost
unapologetically lingering
on every window. How

ordinary it is to be broken
by tenderness in such chill.
The secret is a door handle,
then trees blue and spindly

in the cold air. A generous
lean into another's body.
Perhaps a song still echoing
from the charmed moments.

Already the current in which
floats the boat bearing
the heart seems smoother.
Know that the river is simply

rehearsing a marathon to be run
again and again. Sometimes so much
is offered before the sun beckons
the latticework of ice to join this flow.

Half Ghost

Everything's turning to tin so soon
this morning: the frozen wheat field, the earth
of the footpath, the half ghost of my heart.
I'm out in the street like a frost-pain dream,
bare-faced and stiff, but alive. I'm trotting
by the shop first, by the dead oak tree next.
I'm turning warm. A couple of birds leap
into frosty, big-bellied brooks as if
seeing the tail of a bad-tempered dog.
My feet shouting back at their call. The hours
break like mist on the early morning grass.
And though I'm suffering, I feel the world
can't ever end now. I'm happy, flesh hot
as a stove, soul coming to a whistle.

Strange Factories

From how small
a split will we
supernova

when a constellation
of gears spins
and gnashes within us?

We are strange factories
of heat and light.
Sometimes nothing

seems as fragile
as the motions
of our machinery.

Listen to the howl
of our engines.
Listen for the click

of two cogs
not quite meeting.
Time shears us cleanly

but not every force
is as forgiving.
There are hidden points

of failure within us.
Each memory of you,
I've made by burning

a wavering match
in front of my teeth.
I wanted to be a vessel

for fire. I wanted
to be held by your
gravity, aflame

and dying like the sun.

II

Always, the runner is haunted. His race is a form of flight—
from himself, from the mediocrity of society,
from a lugubrious backstory.

—Sam Shaw

Tributaries

i.

It doesn't matter whether the river has a name like birdsong

or that when spoken   it causes the tongue to escape teethridge

and flood the air with honeycombed sound

Because the river dances   like the sun on a broken mirror

and wants to break every stone it crosses   So I chip and scatter

mountains from myself   I fracture   and wait

I become the earth's shiver as the river falls over it

But every mountain will fail to offer any resistance when the river

smashes its banks   I know the river runs as easily as a breath

from my spillway lungs   I can't stop the river

any more than I can stop the unraveling of steel in the forge

It will always be both honey and hammer

It plies its course   and all I really want is to run the same path

Every time I speak the river's name   the wind takes my words

because what the river made was not for me   but for itself

47

ii.

Three hours after our cheers   joined the acrid smoke

of burning tables   curtains   doors ripped from hinges

and one orange hazard cone swiped from the pothole it covered

in the street   heat mushrooming into the tender canopy

of early summer   we ran   fell into the hole of night

and finally slept   the feverish kind of sleep only possible

when every beam of light   crawling across the ceiling passes

like a wave or the turn of a page

Burnt varnish and polyester pungent in our hair

Stinging eyes squeezed shut   so as to sleep off

not only the voracious flames   but the miles of cropland

passed in the immeasurable night   The same dark storefronts

lining every prairie town   Traffic lights always flashing red

across parade-wide main streets   Charcoal kettles planted

like cannonballs near the porches of clapboard split-levels

The river and the old railways   spanning it flickering like dying incandescent bulbs   So many little cities

of distant floodlights   We have left the bonfire still breathing

somewhere along the river's shore   We do this for its own sake

for its light   for the crack and snap of its ravings

iii.

Someone's carried a wishbone to the end of the sky

where a vein of dawn gleams like a filament

of smoke   Only this bone also murmurs my name

and bears witness when I mistake my mouth

for river wetness   soaking every hour east

of sierra-chewed sky   There's always one last roll call

before the bounce of asphalt dislodges days

passed as riddles   This rhythm is an escape route

is it not   lifting me from the menace of mountains

from gnashing dust   from gin-veined monologues

from streams of names   and the business of being too early

I've spent many miles watching reflections rattle

between streaked horizons   the night glued together by hindsight

my body becoming a burst of numbers

while streetlights smolder   in every direction

iv.

On streets angled like shattered glass   a twenty-four hour

song of shoe-sole syncopations   rivers its way between

brownstones and fills the air with something more than dust

The language of drill and jackhammer   of horn and hum

of galaxies of fluorescents   and melted strings of neon

An endless babble   without breath   I'm nearly lost

within this concrete cacophony   But it's always a turn

sharper and sharper each time taken   that leads towards

the recognition that everything is born already as an echo

and echoed within itself   I finally catch myself

among the fish-eyed schools of window reflections   as if

another person   slower   smaller

almost an imperceptible nothing   A mote over miles of asphalt

v.

What if touching your collarbone becomes like walking

down the broken sidewalk   my outstretched hand grazing

to raw red on a brick wall   I will know then

that time can be a gift   as long as it's not measured

as distance   May I never keep

my arms at my sides rather than wear them down

on you   Besides   when were we ever tougher

than clay   Yes   there was a time when we were like sand

escaped from the hourglass   Free to etch our designs

and then scour them away   Then we became the river

that flooded the fields   greening crooked

trees after the long winter   I always forget

how this transformation began

III

The history of running is mostly away,
not chasing but chased...
                    —Elizabeth Langemak

Why Do We Bathe in Miles of Dust?

Because it's a type of hunger
that drives the small changes
in ourselves? Hair of wasps,
pit-mine eyes, sapwood bones.

What if we fill our bellies so fully
that we begin to chew the sun,
which in turn chews us
like a rough road through a rubber tire?

Will the mirror then expose
the give-and-mostly-take nature
of our bodies? There will be a time
when we no longer remember

north, south, the race to the dollop
of light at the day's end.
It's not that we've been taught
to fear nightfall, but rather

the moment when our machinery
hesitates and begins to run
in reverse. There will be a point
when the mirror tells us that,

really, we've been consuming
ourselves, leaving nothing except
salt-sweetened scars traced
like fragile mountains across our skin.

It's hunger that cannot be satiated
even with bright knives of open sky.
We'll feast on gravel until we lie
scattered like fallen birds in the fields.

High Water

Fireflies knife the skin of night
and dare a showy waltz.
Their flight patterns dissolve
like sugar over the garden.
Hollowed and again reading the ice
in my drink, I watch the fireflies
momentarily re-green the dark tree line
one pinpoint of light at a time.
But the night is a sea,
its darkness liquid.
It pours back over the insects,
refilling each spot of waning light.
So when I'm watching the fireflies,
the hours softening as my melting ice shifts
and collapses into itself,
I'm really watching the miles between us
drown. Every time the shadows anchor
themselves under the leaves
in the absence of wind, I'm reminded
of the night's high-water mark
and that there will be no crossing.

Do You Remember the Storm

Do you remember the storm
we saw shoving the whole lake
upon the rock-jutted shore?
Lichens burned red with wetness.
Evergreens ached against the wind.
Rain seemingly sprang from the ground
as everywhere hung
the delirious sound of hillsides of water
detonating against the rocks.
I intended to tell you
that I would have sacrificed
the entirety of that shoreline to the waves
to watch the cliffs lose
their pretensions of timelessness
and collapse slowly into the cold water.
But I imagined you'd turn away,
uninterested in the waves' eventual triumph,
unaware that to me, you were the storm.

Ice Bright in the Harbor

Ice bright in the harbor heals
into a flat field. It complains
underfoot, gnawing its stony
scars as if scrapping a bone clean

against the teeth on the edge
of the world. Sometimes nobody
is around to hear this. The ice
simply speaks to the wind.

There have been times I've heard
this hidden shout, snapped
like a branch, held like a snarl,
emanating from somewhere deep

within where two sheaves can't help
but cease holding together.
A deep tear lets in no light.
But a crack, which forms like a tear,

is an opening able to be closed
again. Sometimes it's not surprising
when a window of sky opens
on the surface like a wound.

Personal Best: A Door Opens

A mirage is born
in front of the eyes

as the wind across
the body speaks

its empty truth.
Breath, a roar

in the ears, hides
an entire land of want.

A door opens
but remains unseen.

The mind floats
into a pinhole

of silvery light.
Limbs are bound

and pulled under
heavy water.

There is no mercy
to the shore

when diving into the waves
feels the same as falling

from the sky.
A door once open,

remains. The body
will remember this,

even when
door after door

swings open,
the last never entered.

Fields

No dusk snaps its possibilities back
from the fire. No dawn tapers its doorway

to finger width. It's living that cuts back
the fields of us. Hours full of ritual,

full of desire in knots of wildflowers.
We fail to grasp them all. Not that we try

anyway, too busy wearing the patterns
of the wind into the soles of our feet.

Sometimes it seems there's only one pathway
through the fields. I've left so much in the slick,

trampled grass that all I can think to do
is blame the minutes themselves. I spoke of

this once to you. But the clock kept moving.
Fire burning. I kept running into the wind.

When Our Home No Longer Whispers

When our home no longer whispers
of sweat and body shadows,
will we listen to the settling dust
and know the smoky touch

of the smothered days on our shoulders?
In time, this will all turn to ash.
Yes, I mean both us and the wood
and plaster of our home. We'll surrender

to the wind and whir of a flip-book
of easily forgotten moments. I can never tell
which is more important: the flash
of images or the airy oblivion of the space

between them. I'm learning to turn
each page as if the paper were a bridge
on which you stand. Floating slowly down
into the abyss is every little thing

that once tethered me to you. Torn
bread. Tea leaves. The pith of grapefruit.
A house is held together by little
things until time also eats them away.

Eventually, like the slow topple
of a wall or like tired bodies
gently colliding, every page
will have unfurled into the last.

The Softest Things

Sometimes the softest things break
the bones of twilight. I watch the rain

goose bump the street from the window
over the porch. Blue-black flood

flashing with tiny yellow crowns—
the sodium-vapor glow of streetlights

catching the splashdown of droplets.
Neither taillights nor high beams

will-o-the-wisp through the downpour.
No life other than the traffic signal

muttering its colors to the rippling gutters.
They say that solitude can be hard—

by which they mean difficult. It's more
soft than anything else—a blood-buzz

jacket easily worn and quietly warming the
shoulders like the memory of another's breath.

Do You Blame the Morning

Do you blame the morning
for the tendrils of smoke

across the field?
Or the broken triangles of light

for falling like prayers

over the dragon's teeth
of icy tall grass?

A day slowly yawns
into existence.

Ligaments crack
open like doors.

The vapor of our breath
hanging like fruit

on greasy windows,
nostrils finding skin's sweetness

and the charcoal bite of air.

Let me ask,

how does the earliest light
always know to fill the deepest faults

that run the earth?

We've drawn such ragged terrain

that I sometimes expect
wells full of ink

to greet me when I wake.

Instead, the morning
wrings us through its cold prism,

stretches us over its knife.

We've let every incomplete map
guide us to this hour,

and now we find only smoldering char
to remind us of the rare heat

that pulled at us stronger
than a warm vein of sun.

Will the Nearly Broken World Understand

how we each speak with an empty heart?
Remember, our tongues are bullets. Our
hands are black from rifle-fire. We eat
the still-hot soil after we burn the animal
inside our skin. We walk to the water
with this bitter taste and find that iron
floats. It blossoms in our mouths, then it
hovers weightless in a deepening lake.
Wolves have built a honeycomb island
of skulls out alone in the water. There
they cry and sing, howling in a garden of
bone. They tear wildflowers from our
bodies like sinews. Thirst for meat and
marrow, the soft tomatoes of our ribs.
You mend me with sutures of real grass
when they've finished and before they
come again. This could be seen as a cold
kind of beauty, but instead I dream only
that these bloody hours will finally end.

To Feed the Fire

your voice was the axe that flattened the forest to feed the fire

grief unfurls like paper tossed into the furnace, you tell me

it's okay to lose my heart amongst the trees, tremor

with the missing scent of your skin as I wait for the bruised

sky to be revealed, run like a tongue across a threadbare shirt

the roughness of hunger spilling against my teeth, shivering

like last winter's ghost down my spine or the canopy of ash

trees against the steadiness of a chopping blade

you tell me that we both should've known better, I cannot change

how quickly we fill the forest floor or how deeply

the flames must reach to open the volumes within us

Who Will Play the Song of Catastrophe

when it's our voices instead
that boomerang between silence

and the shattering of fiction?
We're drowning in the high

harsh vowels of denial, no
longer hearing music or truth

anywhere but at the land's end.
We know that the sea can carve

iron as if it were sugar cubes
and that bones always whirl

back up from the carbon black sea
floor. We study these ghosts

as they approach our tumultuous
coast, before we feed them again

to the eager mouths of waves,
just to watch them roll in the surf

back to our feet. The water
always returns our sins.

Pinhole Sunrise

All my senses are sucker-punched by the cold
as a pinhole sunrise bleeds a muted horizon
onto the street. I'm vainly trying to praise the notion
of the bursting heart and start the frozen car.
We wait outside for the engine block to warm
because the seats are unbearable and solid
as cured concrete. The car exhaust smells of celery
and maple syrup. My words have been billowing
into corkscrews of fog that catch unacknowledged
in the skeletal canopy of leafless branches. The wind
clamors like an orchestra, playing for its audience
the more orderly mathematics of hoar frost
and scattering my voice like the whips of snow
that snake across the half-plowed pavement.
Every breath of cold air viciously plays the accordion
of our lungs. The crisp edge of single digits
bulldozes through us. Even if I could hush
the wind and stop its cold fingers from pulling us
apart, we'd still fall into silence to watch the violet sky
pink itself with new light. We'd still scrape
our boots against frost-locked rock salt. The array
of our footprints, never quite overlapping, would still spell
out what we aren't saying to each other. What our lips
always fumble in these smudged and lonely hours.

The Most Difficult Thing

what if the most difficult thing I do is carry your voice with me

nobody resembles a god as much as the souvenir-seeker

cradling one trinket all the way home just to shatter it

on the walls, I'm sure it's been written that joy can be a brute

and that the truth is like climbing sheer cliffs rising over a vast sea

my chest filling with something cloudless and inevitable

as you keep calling me your map to everywhere, and I'm sure

that this too can be called noble, but I don't believe you

Shadeless Roads

The sweat-burned shoulders
of shadeless roads

call to us,

our bodies buzzing
with a thousand wrong numbers.

We spend miles
carving ourselves with daggers
of vertigo to answer them.

Horseflies smacking our skin
like hail,

ankles grinding
like pestles into mortars,

an animal sun
growling its heat into our skulls.

Sometimes we must know
what shape the end of hunger

will reveal in us.

Sometimes need is a cannibal

and we slice
one last sun-shredded piece

off of ourselves,
stumbling hollow and mute

onto the concrete
of our front stoop.

There we unravel like trees into dirt.

There, as we sink

our teeth with a boot-in-mud squelch
into the wet hearts

of tomatoes,
we finally find

a brief tempering of appetite.

The soft dial tone of sunset
melting into us.

The Early Hours

The only island of light, a sandwich shop
      slipped between city brownstones, shines

welding-arc bright against the night.
      An oasis of color. Buzz-song of phosphor.

The shop withstands the pig-iron grayness
      of quiet streets where coal-seam shadows

stretch between lampposts and bare trees.
      Checkerboard tiles glare from its windows.

In the shop there is music: hissing oil,
      wax paper crinkling between fingertips,

the whirl of dropped coins settling
      into their shadows on the floor.

We yawn and slump onto a red tabletop,
      our hunched shoulders shedding snow

and other bits of grief like the neon
      relish and mustard-bound clumps of onion

that have fallen and made little mounds
      around our elbows. Our seats offer a view

of distant towers rising over tar-stained
      rooftops. Below, tire tracks are forming

calligraphy in the light snow. We try
      but cannot read it. The early hours continue

to crash against the shop like storm-
        churned swells against a lighthouse.

We can only watch ourselves waver
        and melt over the dark sea of plate glass.

The Late Hours

When the late hours stick to this city like honey
what little comforts do we haul up from the wells

of urgency within us as thousands of windowpanes
blaze like the refractory bricks in a hot furnace,

gobs of incandescent light falling again and again
onto the blue-gray street? Like a copper plate,

everything is eventually smothered with boneblack
ink. Even the aching orange horizon is brushed

with the inescapable tar of night. Listen,
you can hear the last gasps of gentleness

as the lip of land melts into the sky
which melts into the empty shapes

of unnamed tomorrows. Scars of late-night
neon morph weeds and grass into slender fish

around our ankles. Broken-bone trees reach
for our faces. The street looms as if a gulf.

There may be nothing that fills us as much
like cold water as when our way home transforms

into an indecipherable puzzle, every angle
of everything dismantled by hidden hands.

But if we press ourselves into the intricacies
of the smallest shadows, we'll etch our path

through the darkness, a flurry of moonrises
with our every moment. We'll trace the constellations

of gravel spangling each other's backs and always
remember where to spark an unquenchable light.

Snapped Collarbone

The sweet scent of leaf decay
brings all kinds of phantoms to the hilltop.
First, bewilderment.
An uneasy sense of movement
without effort, without the rush
of air across skin. Instinctive twitch
as a net of mosquitos drapes over
my face and arms. An unseen buzzing
seeping into me. Other sounds
come one by one. Anonymous crunch
of rubber over gravel through trees.
The sandy sigh of grass against
rock and broken asphalt. I watch
the treetops sway, the sunlight almost
becoming a burden, until suddenly
I need to get somewhere I don't remember.
Like I've missed
an appointment I never made.
A cold universe begins to flare
within me. Galaxies, entire systems
of red giants and white dwarfs and
zombie stars consuming other suns
plump into huge masses, burn brighter
and brighter until they've even set fire
to the emptiness that howls
between my memories
and the smallest parts of the world.
Air sticks to sweat.
I want to let gravity cascade me
down the ravines, through the trees.
I want to escape the exposed root,
the impact of shoulder on earth,
the consequences of milliseconds.

A hum escapes my throat.
It grows and becomes a song
I haven't heard since I last lay
in the grass staring at the sky, wondering
how to undo what cannot be undone.

On the Shore of the Lake, I Stare into the Midnight Sky

Another satellite passes. A grain of salt
sliding across the smudge of galaxy.
But for the slap of lake on rock, silence.

Ennui

Always, the body will gnaw its lonesome
way toward the invisible grove of
ennui. Toward the shadows tumbling from
the mountains teething into the sun's path.
Still, many points of joy are allotted
along this passage. Music that quakes ribs.
Late spring rain tinseling the trees. The heart,
a postcard of warm lamplight. It's never
just the depth of a lake masked by snow or
the slow mud-death of a trampled meadow
that wears down the already worn, covers
tracks already covered. The body will
misremember this. Believing, perhaps,
in spirals. That there might be a way back.

Where Have Your Wanderings Finally Brought You?

I wondered, finger-tracing the crease-cut
roadmap you flattened in with your letter.

You spoke of fields thorned with iron
shavings, broken railway ties soaked

sweet with creosote, and mounds of soot
like cooked fleas alongside faint trails of ruts

and weeds. You said you thought that the tons
of barkless trees were stacks of sun-bleached bones.

And that you didn't know what to do
with them, the mounds and the bones,

but you figured one would become the other
soon anyway. You wrote that when you looked

into the gray canals from empty bridges,
only the famished sky glared back.

The last ember of recognition nearly drowning
before you realized that this was home.

Lights

Lights wander like cotton in the window
of my squint.
                 Hundreds.
                              Thousands.
                                               Short-lived stars
fumbling into the harsh night
to tally the final business.

But the minutes rebel,
sorting themselves into hard blues and greens.

A forest of concrete. Sidewalk shining
like milky glass.

My body continues
to chop a line through the air.

The sky toes
over the horizon.

Time sings its song,
and I've become a disciple of this

confusing orbit of myself.
The lights blossom and

I emerge as an echo.
Never do I catch the previous me.

Tipping Point

Can you distinguish between the loss of time
and the neat rows of the same plastic homes
staring each other down across the bright

green quilts of new, thirsty grass pulled up
to their sun-bleached concrete foundations,
the same dark windows, the same unstained

driveways with their garage doors closed
against the unbroken prairie wind? Whole
years have been taken from us out here.

The fields have petrified into ribbons
of asphalt. Air almost glacial now yields
to the tang of fresh oil in the sun.

Even the yellow-gray dirt seems impossibly
old, cut by rain into smiling ridges. I can't follow
the timeline of such changes. Imagine, these hills

were once crowned by nothing. I used to chase
seconds along the shoulders of open roads.
Every stride questioning which frequency

my lungs must match to align me with
the pulse of dust kicked up from the roadside.
I have been sheared to near nothingness,

a wire-whip sapling bent in the wind.
I don't recall the smooth motion of either
the minute or hour hands. All I see now are lights

flickering on and off in those photocopied
subdivisions. I know there is a tipping point
like age or the same story retold a thousand times

that leaves you in these places, a muddy stream
in a hidden canyon curling again and again
around mossy stones until it goes dry.

About the Author

Dane Hamann works as an editor and indexer for a textbook publisher in the southwest suburbs of Chicago. He received his MFA in Creative Writing from Northwestern University, after which he served as the poetry editor of TriQuarterly for over five years. His chapbook *Q&A* was published by Sutra Press and his micro-chapbooks have been included in multiple Ghost City Press Summer Series.

www.ingramcontent.com/pod-product-compliance
Lightning Source LLC
Chambersburg PA
CBHW020214090426
42734CB00008B/1063